THE EXQUISITE PAIN OF THE UNREQUITED

POEMS

J. R. ROGUE

This is a work of fiction. Names, characters, places, and incidents are a
product of the author's imagination. Locales and public names are
sometimes used for atmospheric purposes. Any resemblance to actual
people, living or dead, or to businesses, companies, events, institutions, or
locales
is completely coincidental.

J.R. Rogue
PO Box 984
Lebanon, MO 65536
www.jrrogue.com
contact@jrrogue.com

CONTENTS

For every lover who has
tasted the unrequited kind,
too many times.

PART 1
THE STAIN SOULMATES LEAVE BEHIND

ENTRY 1

I collect my

weakness in jars

& they sure look

pretty on my shelf

the one with your

flawless little name

on the label,

will never collect dust

I always pull it down

& my thumbs wipe it clean

& my arms pull it close

& my silly sad sanity slips

& I pretend

you love me too

ENTRY 2

this

morning

you splayed your fingers

on the tile as

I pressed into

your tired shoulders.

I watched some of the world

roll down your spine

with the shower spray.

you moaned lightly

& I pursed my lips.

tomorrow

morning

I will practice not loving you.

I am living,

no longer

      lingering in what

        I hoped we could be.

I am calm,

no longer frantic—

fumbling for

    the fantasy of us

that was always floating

    in the peripheries

     of my vision.

I am...

  almost-acceptance.

I never asked for this.

no, I never asked to

fall in love with you.

I never asked for my world

to be flipped around,

for hearts to be broken

simply because you exist.

for me to find

a new place to sleep at night,

& for most of those

nights to be restless.

for friends & family

to question my sanity.

for me to ache most days,

questioning it myself.

for you to kiss me,

putting every past lover to shame.

for your skin to be the

only softness capable of bringing

forth my own.

almost lovers

full mouth kisses

empty promises

dropped silently

into the bathroom trash

my scent scrubbed

off your exhausted sex

I clench my eyes

& pretend I don't

hear you

retreating from

my life

call me "friend" again

&

watch my eyes

as all the light

exits the room

ENTRY 6

you draw my heartache

on the side of your black coffee

cup, two blocks from the coast

every other Wednesday or so.

oh you love the lost, too much.

I think I can feel it

most days

in the in-between;

you spell my name in strange

ways— *b l a m e.*

I begged you for a last kiss.

I begged you &

I got it.

I begged &

I can still taste your pity.

I spent most of last night

on that concrete slab in

my back yard I named

"the chill spot."

no one comes over,

no one smokes out

there or passes my

bottle back to me.

I set it in the grass,

& pretend that was

my last *last* sip.

then I marry my lips to

the rim again & fall over

laughing.

I wonder if my mouth
tasted different to you.

not like a woman
of thirty who had
fallen into
convenience five or
six times & called it "love."

maybe I just tasted
like something new
to write about.
a handful of fucks
& I am born again,
believing in things
I never actually believed in.

soulmates &
stained bedsheets,
your letters next to mine
on locks locked over
a Paris bridge we will
never see.

I put my mouth to

your aching neck,

I tasted salt & boredom.

I told myself it

was a second cousin

to love

& close enough.

well, maybe in our

next life.

for now I'll just be

that thirty-year-old

mistake you write

about on your off

days.

The pads of my feet

made love to

the street at a brisk pace—

to keep up with the strides

of the stranger who promised

to take me away from it all

for a while.

a shot of regret,

a vow to get

over you.

the rain crawled

from its concrete

grave to my knees

that no longer

prayed for your affections.

I believe the sky is crying for

us & what we will never be.

DRINKING GAMES

my elbow is raw.
my index finger worries it,
attempting to scrape
the regret off before
it lands on that
familiar bar top.

moonshine cherry kisses.
the part of me that
misses
you,
stored away for a later day.

I swear I'll win this game
one of these days.

I twisted my ankle last night.

I broke a heel.

(new pumps.

what a bitch.)

faces blur under sin city lights.

liquor & laughter lingers

& I don't know how I

crawled back to this bed alive.

the Vegas heat beyond

the Venetian blinds calls to me,

so I count the bruises

& ignore her plea.

(I know tonight will

be rinse & repeat.)

I only wanted a goodbye.

now I'm crossing

another lover

off my list.

his initials are carved next to yours.

his letters aren't nearly as deep.

IN MEMORIAM

who will deliver my eulogy?

I can see judgement,

stares,

mourners.

falling for you was a sin,

& small towns remember them.

you see, they have vaults filled

with transgressions.

my name,

red ink.

& the truth is,

I care not if they forgive me.

my brief moment with you,

I shall never regret.

PART 2
FIGHT OR FLIGHT

DEPARTURES & ARRIVALS

the tide is low on Tuesdays.

I think Poseidon knows.

the jagged rock

is always dry after I clock out

& walk the five blocks to

where we kissed for the

first time.

my feet

whisper hello & goodbye to

the water's surface

as I look for your face

in the sky.

you flew away

on a Tuesday.

I'm sure you'll fly

home then too.

BAGGAGE UNCLAIMED

I pawned my heart for a
red eye flight.
I lost reciprocal &
requited.

I was too busy licking my
wounds on my layover.

now I have nothing for him &
he knows it.

DELAYS & CANCELLATIONS

I flew away on a tiny jet plane.

I flew away from your

black hole quiet.

there's un-forgiveness

climbing up your spine.

I had to go before it covered

your eyes.

it's turning cold again in the city

& I see

your silhouette on all the streets

you've never visited.

this is a kind of missing I have

never known.

did you feel it that day?

I placed my fingertips on your

forearm

    & everything lined up.

my soul harmonized to yours.

there's a tether connecting us.

it moves

under city streets &

mid-America fields;

from the tips of my toes

to your leaving heel.

I'm by the phone waiting

for forgiveness.

waiting for you to

be ready.

waiting.

all my life I'll be

waiting for you.

HOLDING PATTERN

I kept waiting for him

to want me to return.

I didn't have my fill.

I didn't feel my desire dwindling.

I'd fly home just to run some

errands & tidy my room,

just to fly

back to him again.

I'd spend my last dollar.

I'd sell all my possessions.

but he never asked.

perhaps my

memory began to fade as soon

as I took my seat on the plane.

perhaps 70-some hours & change

was all he really needed of me.

perhaps I will always fly

for the heartbreak-kids.

THE DEVIL, DENIAL, & DAY TERRORS

11:11. *make a wish.*

I bruised my wrist.

slam slam slam on the bar

another shot please?

"it's happy hour somewhere,"

the Devil whispered

in my ear as

he pushed my hair aside &

told me the widower by the sea

may love me again.

in seven or so Sundays

his lies tasted best chased

with salt & sour smiles.

in the meantime, I've been
sleepwalking from
strangers' beds.

tell me his deceit will
blossom into half-truths.

tell me I can make
my way back to you.

SHALLOW DEPTHS

you create a spark—

with your touch,

with all you do,

& who you are.

your lips. your leaving.

Lichtenberg scars

& heart bleeding.

still, she reads Bukowski

to impress you.

to prove her depths.

the kind you don't swim in—

the one thing she can't grasp.

but who am I to say a thing?

when I am always

standing in the rain,

on the nights I,

too,

hear your name.

ANCHOR EYES

I said it in the beginning

       to whomever

would listen

that I wasn't the kind of woman

who could hold the attention

of a man like that

       for more than a few days

  maybe he saw anchors in my eyes

I need to know his beauty exists

out there

& I hope no woman

ever tries to tame him

I'll compare the rest to him,

I will

his presence is essential to me
       & I never lived
until I knew him

DRIFTWOOD

this bar is a harbor,

so I'll dock my soul for the night.

you know I'm looking for you,

most moons,

you do not show.

don't worry, I'll take a shot for you

& wait for you to

drift back

too.

PART 3

THE LIES WE TELL

PART 1

"I want you. I miss you.

I have fallen so fucking hard for you."

I pull the pillow tight against

my tired skull,

but still I hear the soft drop of

his words awakening

my skin—flushed ruby.

I shut my eyes

& count our moments.

"you can break me open.

if anyone can. it will be you."

"you make me feel things

I've never experienced."

"please, don't go anywhere."

the streetlight is winking at me.
it's smirking,
beyond my broken blinds.

"why do we lie to ourselves?"
it laughs.

broken hearts,

& my name jotted

on the dotted line.

a new lease & a new life.

a new identity with a new possibility.

plane tickets, your mouth,

& tangled bed sheets.

I wrecked it all

for the chance to touch you,

to love you without remorse.

in return I received your silence,

& a harsh reality.

the fantasy of me,

was sold easily.

the flesh-&-bone me,

was discarded wordlessly.

I'll never fall for a lie

like that one again.

I'll never fall for words like yours.

I'll never weep for

someone who didn't care

enough to tell me why.

PART 3

tell me the-day-in
and-day-out with you
is horrid.
tell me you leave the
toilet seat up and
you forget to clean
the wax from your ears.

tell me I'll become uninterested
and really, you're quite a dull lover.

tell me you will
stop holding my hand
and your fascination
with me will fade.

tell me the soft tone of your
voice will float away,
replaced by silence and
bored bedroom eyes.

tell me anything you wish.
anything to kill my desire.

I romance you,
and you regret me.

lend a hand and help me stand
with you, on the same page.

PART 4

my favorite moments
were the ones
I would allow myself to
chew on the lie.

it tasted like blood red cherries
in the summer
as it swam around my gums.

I let it stain my fingers &
the edges of my t-shirt as
I pulled it over my head
& pulled you closer.

I knew you were
merely a moment-man,

so I closed my eyes &

    enjoyed the ones you

    gave me.

PART 5

you said you were falling;
I said the same.
it was beauty & it
was smiles & it was
nothing I had ever known.

then, suddenly, it was
friendship with a pinch
or two of flirting.

& my fear
turns me to stone.

we both know
I'll never ask why.

YOUR SADNESS

the beautiful man who lives

by the bay,

wants to give me a chance

a chance to be

the smiling-kind

the happy-little-

shining-kind

he wants to release

the ink from my eyes,

to drain you from my veins

he has a glossy little

two story

storybook

haven where

I can heal in

the beautiful man who lives

by the bay, no, I can't have him

I'm in love with my madness

I cannot consume his resplendence

I only want you;

your lips &

your beautiful

sadness

SWAN SONG

we write sad songs better

than the rest.

our niche. our place in this mess.

let me say goodbye to you?

let me stretch it out?

a day or two,

the boardwalk,

& the Atlantic.

neon orbs painting your skin

on mine

for a while.

touch me. make me sing.

don't worry that I'll hold on.

don't worry that I'll pull hope

from your parted lips.

I am resigned. I am resolute.

I won't cry this time.
not while you're
standing in my room.
not while your gaze
is turned my way.

I'll save it for a rainy day.
& you can go back to
acting as though there was
never anything between us
in the first place.

SIX DEGREES

the morning sun

covered you in a canary canvas.

so I drew nearer to you

& drew lines

all over your feather skin.

connect the dots.

between our past

& our meeting,

& our fall

& your leaving.

yes.

you were beneath me,

but so long gone.

PART 4
PAPER CUTS

PART 1

I'm in love with a coward

& a thief.

a romantic with these damned

despondent eyes

I cannot break away from.

I plunged my fist through his

paper thin promises.

he blinked. he ran.

an inch of something akin

to forever was inked in my iris.

he clenched. he ran.

& I will never

forgive him.

PART 2

I have these pretty paper men

following me from tree to tree.

they want to love me.

they are pretty.

pretty on paper.

long legs for chasing

& strong arms for turning me

to face them.

I bet they would feel nice,

bare & breathless, by my side.

but they, are not you.

they can't make me sing

the way you used to.

WILLOW WEEPING

I remember our

last kiss,

under that

old willow

tree.

you left us

both

weeping.

AMNESIA

he took me three times last night

& once this morning.

the things he whispered...

his future plans for my flesh;

ropes,

   & knots,

     & exposure.

I reddened.

I heated.

he pressed his lips to my

core &, for a moment,

I forgot your name.

THE HEAVY

I can feel the heavy.

I am still wrapped in my sheets

& I feel it.

not the heavy I want;

the weight of you above me

the feel of your tender back beneath

my wanting fingertips...

no, not that.

it's the weight of you deciding

I wasn't much more than

a silly crush

& a passing fancy.

that's what I feel.

I feel it.

MICROSCOPIC MOMENTS

it's okay,

it is.

it's okay

that you do not

love me.

I am lucky,

I am.

I am lucky

that for a fleeting moment

you thought

maybe you could.

PART 5
RETURN TO SENDER

LETTER 1

I wrote you a letter.

I wrote down everything
I could never
find the courage to tell you—
how your silence splits me,
how numb I am now,
how I am letting go.

when I came home today,
I noticed
the mailman had missed
the envelope with your name
scribbled in my sloppy scrawl.

so, I dropped it in the trash.

maybe there are some things

the universe doesn't

want you to know yet.

LETTER 2

I want to write a poem.

I want to write a poem about

how I feel,

how I felt,

wrapped in my fresh sheets

today,

mid-day,

blinds shut,

phone on silent.

I want to write a poem.

I want to write a poem about my

tears & the red of my face

& the black of my heart.

I want to write a poem

but I,

    am too frozen.

they will write stories about how

we found each other.

(the kind that piss people off.

because they don't believe it's true.

because they want it for themselves.)

& I will write stories about

how we lost each other.

(because that's the part I will never

get over. that's the part I know best.)

& he will write stories

about the delicate

moments in

between.

(in those you will find my

love for him.)

LETTER 4

I ache.

my temple

pounds.

I see stars,

but they don't glitter

the way they did last night

under the downtown lights.

my mouth,

an arid arena.

words never said to you

compete with the taste

of him

still

lingering

in my throat.

PHANTOM LIMB

he said I had Gotham eyes,

then he bit my lip

& smacked my ass.

he didn't draw blood

& he didn't draw me out

in the way he had hoped.

not in the way you did.

you wound my dark hair

around your fist &

made me cry out.

it was with the same force

he used on me.

but behind yours was

a wildness I couldn't find anywhere

but in the depths of your eyes

& within

the way you shivered when my

lips grazed your neck.

I felt safe in

your unknown.

I was forever falling

into you, even in the arms of others.

LIPSTICK & ILLUSIONS

you bewitch me.

my lipstick stains

have become prayers.

my fingertips

parade all over pleasant

men who *lovelovelove*

my resenting flesh.

it is not you who touches me

on Sunday mornings.

I kneel beside

foreign beds

& beg them to

forfeit this ill illusion.

they do not feel as you do.

they take the magic you

left & dim me in

their dim rooms,

as I hide **lastlastlast** tears.

CODE BLUE

I feel November,

when I lie on the operating table.

I stretch myself out;

shoulder blades—

lonely capsized mountains.

vertebrae—

a sting.

my heels—

pressed.

I cut myself down the middle.

one long incision.

the shock has me numb.

I cut out the love

that remains for you.

I place it in the gun metal
bin next to my limp wrist.
discarded.

I stitch myself up.
your favorite song plays over the
speaker in the waiting room.
I hum your lonely tune.
I wipe you from my cheeks.
your salt, your letters.

maybe it's the chill in the room.
maybe it's not you,
rolling around in my wounds.

maybe this is
the last time, too.

J.R. Rogue first put pen to paper at fifteen after developing an unrequited high school crush and has never stopped writing about heartache. She has published multiple volumes of poetry and novels. Her work has been recognized with three Goodreads Choice Awards nominations, a testament to the impact of her work on readers.

In addition to her writing, J.R. Rogue is a certified yoga teacher with additional certification in Yoga Nidra and Trauma-Informed Yoga. She is passionate about mindfulness and meditation and is studying Foundations in Meditation. Furthermore, J.R. Rogue has been sober from alcohol since January 1st, 2020, a personal achievement that she is proud of and that has strengthened her commitment to mindfulness and wellness.

J.R. Rogue resides in a small town in the Midwest with her family, where she enjoys a peaceful life reading and telling stories.

You can find important links and information here. Join her mailing list to keep up with everything she's working on.

www.jrrogue.com
contact@jrrogue.com

instagram.com/authorjrrogue
threads.net/@j.r.rogue
facebook.com/jrrogueauthor
tiktok.com/@jenro501
amazon.com/J.-R.-Rogue
bookbub.com/authors/j-r-rogue
pinterest.com/rogueauthor

ALSO BY J. R. ROGUE

Romance

MUSE & MUSIC SERIES

Breaking Mercy

Burning Muses

Background Music

Blind Melody

SOMETHING LIKE LOVE SERIES

I Like You, I Love Her

I Love You, I Need Him

I Like You, I Hate Her

Romantic Suspense

RED NOTE SERIES

The Rebound

The Regret

The Return

Supernatural Suspense

OZARK OMENS SERIES

The Girl Next Door

STANDALONE NOVELS

Kiss Me Like You Mean It

POETRY

GOODREADS CHOICE AWARDS NOMINEES

The Exquisite Pain of the Unrequited

Exits, Desires, & Slow Fires

I'm Not Your Paper Princess

Tell Me Where it Hurts

Dark Mermaid Song

Songs for the Stars

After The Blackout

I'll Be Your Manic Anxiety Queen

Daddy Issues

The Words I Wish You Heard

LETTERS FOR THE UNIVERSE

Poems for the Moon: Vol 1

Poems for the Moon: Vol 2

Poems for the Stars: Vol 1

Poems for the Stars: Vol 2

Poems for the Dawn: Vol 1

Poems for the Dawn: Vol 2